# The Habit of Fire:

*Poems Selected & New*

# The Habit of Fire:

## *Poems Selected & New*

**Judith McCombs**

THE WORD WORKS
**Capital Collection**
WASHINGTON, D.C.

First Edition First Printing
***Habit of Fire: Poems Selected & New***


The WORD WORKS
PO Box 42164
Washington, DC 20015
editor@wordworksdc.com

Cover art: Santa Fe Memories, 36 x 40, acrylic on canvas
by JoAnn Clayton Townsend
Book design, typography by Janice Olson

Library of Congress Number: 2004107206
International Standard Book Number: 0-915380-57-9

# ACKNOWLEDGMENTS

The following poems, sometimes in earlier versions, appeared in these magazines and anthologies:

***Abandon Automobile: Detroit City Poetry 2001:*** "In Praise of the Natural Flowing"; ***ambit:*** "The Observers"; ***Bear Crossings: An Anthology of North American Poets:*** "The Man"; ***th blewointmentpress what isint tantrik speshul:*** "Loving a Mountain"; ***Bridge:*** "Accident, 1946," "Let Us Now Praise," "Preparation"; ***Cabin Fever: Poets at Joaquin Miller's Cabin:*** "Afterwards, You Learn," "Pictures Not in Our Albums"; ***Calyx:*** "Epithet," "Love Poem, Later," "Stories Waiting to Happen"; ***Cancer Poetry Project: Poems by Cancer Patients and Those Who Love Them:*** "Let Us Now Praise"; ***Connections:*** "The Dream"; ***Devil's Millhopper:*** "Making Paths" (Kudzu Honorable Mention); ***end of the world speshul anthology:*** "In the Absence of Humans"; ***A Fierce Brightness: Twenty-Five Years of Women's Poetry:*** "Epithet," "Love Poem, Later"; ***Glass Bell Press Broadsides:*** "The Dream"; ***Grrrrr: A Collection of Poems About Bears:*** "The Man"; ***Hungry as We Are: An Anthology of Washington Area Poets:*** "Epithet"; ***In a Certain Place:*** "The Habit of Fire," "In Praise of the Natural Flowing," "Making Paths," "Territory"; ***Jeopardy:*** "The Table"; ***Leaving the Bough: 50 American Poets of the 80s:*** "Packing In With a Man"; ***Loon:*** "Against Nature," "The Artifact," "The Observers"; ***Lovers and Other Losses: Poems by Seven Women:*** "In the Year of Your Death," "The Inheritor"; ***Modern Poetry Studies:*** "After the Surveyor's Death," "In the Cave," "The Trees in the Peaceable Meadow"; ***Moving Out:*** "You don't like the glaciers we see"; ***Nightsun:*** "The Snake Man Explains"; ***Poet Lore:*** "Hallway"; ***Poetry Northwest:*** "Afterwards, You Learn," "An Old Story," "The Man," "Pictures Not in Our Albums," "Post-Concussion, Breaking Down"; ***Potomac Review:*** "Crossing, 1963," "Leaving the Wilderness Campsite," "Making Paths," "November, Ravine Behind Houses" (Poetry Prize), "Untitled Stone Poem"; ***Prairie Schooner:*** "Exodus," "Fairland Care: Voices, Doors," "Heron in Shadowed Waters"; ***Prism International:*** "Another Untitled Love Poem," "My Father Is Diving," "The Summer Woman"; ***Red Cedar Review:*** "Inheritance," "Photograph Taken at My Father's House," "Untitled Stone Poem," "What are you doing"; ***River Styx:*** "Interrogation," "Territory," "The Traveller"; ***Sisters of the Earth: Women's Prose and Poetry About Nature:*** "The Man"; ***Sow's Ear Poetry Review:*** "Pathways"; ***This Is My Best:*** "The Habit of Fire"; ***Wascana Review:*** "Untitled Nature Poem"; ***Waves*** (Toronto): "The Friend,"

"Packing In With a Man"; ***Weavings 2000: the Maryland Millennial Anthology:*** "Afterwards, You Learn"; ***Winners: A Retrospective of the Washington Prize:*** "Love Poem, Later"; ***WPFW 89.3 FM Poetry Anthology:*** "Territory."

"In Praise of the Natural Flowing" and "The Habit of Fire" appeared first in ***Poetry*** cxxvii, no. 4 (January 1976), 205-7.

"In the Year of Your Death," "The Inheritor," "The Headstone and the Bearer," and "Fragment" won the second Neruda-*Nimrod* prize, judged by William Stafford, and appeared first in *Nimrod's* Awards issue. An earlier version of this book manuscript was a finalist for the Poetry Society of America Alice Fay Di Castagnola Award.

* * *

*for my families*

*with heartfelt thanks to the Michigan writers, the Federal Poets, the Macomb St. group, and the New Roomers, who made these poems better; and to Karren Alenier, Barri Armitage, Dan Minock, Miles David Moore, and Hilary Tham, who made the whole book better.*

# CONTENTS

## *from* Against Nature: Wilderness Poems



## After the Surveyor's Death

## *from* ***Territories, Here & Elsewhere***



## Afterwards

## from *Against Nature: Wilderness Poems*

# Against Nature

Here by the lake and its useless ripples
I'm noticing things, I can't help it
There are relics of insects again in the food
There's a wilderness behind me, I know, I paid
to get out here and it's chock-full of dirt

In a place without gates
how can you open
Without windows what do you see

My habits won't work, out here, and yours
won't either (see, the fishing hook squirms
into your clever opposable thumb)

There's a halo of insects between us and nature

Where you pace has no walls and no corners (how
do you stop) The thickets and mud flats are waiting
Shall we pack up and leave, or join in their tangles

Think of our forebears, building their walls
all over the forest, firing the trees
the beasts and the earth till they choked on fire,
wondering why God had set down flowers
here, in the interminable waste of the forests,
where none but wild animals could ever behold

Think of their counting, alone in the winters,
how many windows, how many acres
imposed on the land, how many cupfuls
of flour, of salt, how many times
this sorting and counting: the last defense
against nature

## The Artifact

He lived on a V of avalanched stone
shed from the cliff, scarcely greened over,
the only levels that the forest left open.
His cabin door framed the enormous white cliff
that was still falling down, a river of stone
aiming for him, and no hump of land
or fence to deflect it. He was never safe
but he didn't get buried when the treed land did.
When he sang from his stoop, or howled at the snow,
his voice went up to a smudge in the cliff,
a dead-black socket, a chimney of emptiness
that swallowed his syllables whole. When he peed
in the drifts his water froze like cheap
yellow beads, like an animal's markings, like his eyes
going tawny from drink. He trapped alone
with no voice but his own to remind him which
wasn't trapped, was him, was his own furry paws
working the traps. While the tallow lasted
he could eat almost anything and not throw it up.
He made good money, he used old lists
to remind him what people did with their money.
Fur money, snow money, money for living
alone like a coot, year after year,
surrounded, until he forgot what it was
to be among people, their quirks and the smell
of their cunning pink hands.

Now his cabin lies rotting in the V of stone
he inhabited. There's a trail for the summer hikers,
and the forest has Indians, hired by the day
to dig rocks from the trail, make the wilderness smooth.
His rafters and roof are gone into mold,
the precious nails stolen. The hikers picnic

on what's left of his logs, eating fresh peaches,
comparing their gear, vaguely aware
that it must have been hard to belong to this place.
From the cabin's doorhole a pink-legged sportsman
measures the cliff, remarks that artifacts
(this cabin, the inhabited site) breed flies.

# The Friend

You are going into the wilderness, O.K., O.K.
Do you mind if I check, have you matches enough,
the heavens might drip? What about mirrors,
do you know how to signal, and suppose the compass
goes out of whack? Have you buttoned your pockets?
You're not a natural-born cave man, you know.
Will you carry I.D.? My book says your maps
can't be relied on. Supposing it snows,
you've heard of crevasses? If you intend to write
(or even to think), where will you sit?
If something comes hunting for you, will you kill it?
You can always eat tree bark, you can always call home
and I'll pay. But what shall I do with your turtle,
in case it escapes? What about mail?
Are you sure you're carrying your own address,
and your three kinds of notebooks to write on—
the used-up, the partly used, and also the new?
I worry about you, uprooted, surrounded
by green things with roots that don't talk
and stone things with no roots, not talking at all.
Are you trying to survive (you know you won't like it,
all by yourself), and how can I get you, out there?

# Loving a Mountain

*for Red Eagle*

## I

Loving a mountain is not
easy. You will have to take it, stone
by stone, into your hands and your skin
and into the space in your head that is prepared
for mountains. You will need a very large
emptiness, a very large need
in yourself: you will have to be willing to move
impediments (your habits of eating, of reason) out.
To encompass a mountain requires
a twat like a horse-collar, an enormous
appetite; the hole in your head will have to be
made larger, by you. (You cannot expect the mountain
to help.) The winds will conspire to trick you,
the lichens shift
under your feet. The trees will ignore you,
the birds throw stones. If you try to move fast, expect
to fall off. You will have to wait till you have become
(in a sense) that mountain.

Loving a mountain is not easy
(or mutual, or useful at all).

## II

You will have to learn how to learn
the slopes and the steepness, the places that welcome
your intrusion, the ponderous folds and wrinkles
where trees clamber upwards. Learn where the mountain
is tired, where it's unwilling to hold any more,
underfoot or over your head. Learn
the days when the ledges are happy and the great folds smile,

basking like pigs in the light. Stop being jealous
of the dust and the fauna: they got here first
and besides have adapted
better than you will: of course the mountain prefers
them. Learn when it wants you
to get off its back: stop staring, stop grabbing,
stop thinking of it.

## III

The mountain is there, a mountain. It is not
inside you. It has all it can do
being a mountain. It does not want
to be loved.
Or, your patience has not been sufficient:
maybe only a glacier could move slowly enough,
carry enough weight, to come to grips
with a mountain. Or maybe the problem is you,
who can't settle for being part of a mountain
in the way that the ignorant tree roots, the insects and pebbles,
are part.
Your expensive techniques of survival,
your comforts, your ideas have cost you
this mountain: go back
where you came from.
Raise parsley,
it's attainable.

Or maybe
(oh day of all blessings) in the back of your head the mountain
will move
lumpishly, creaking like the masts of a distempered ship,
suddenly, ponderously becoming
your mountain.

# Untitled Nature Poem

Nature is not like you and me, dear,
whatever its virtues it doesn't have hands
and it isn't our garden. If the inhabitants
squeak to each other, if the stones understand
what hooks them to earth, that does us no good.
The clever things hide when they hear us, and the rest
move so god-awful slow, we can't notice, or follow.
A strange kind of time is elapsing, outside
of our watches. We can't make the mountains conform
to the lines on our map—they slide in the night
and when we're not looking. Between boulder and boulder,
forest and scree, summit and summit,
there aren't any numbers, only the earth.

We are surrounded
                                        by boulders, by mountains
by passes as high up and as cold as mountains.
This so-called valley was shed from a mountain
and that sky going black up over the summits
has eaten the last of our flares (no answer).

There's a perfect night view of the mountains behind us,
a real panorama, just like the brochures,
but it's bigger and colder and harder than us.
Let's talk about something more human: my hands
in your pockets, you're ticklish, and who left the grease
in the stewpot again, and why is the bedrock
on my side of the tent? My watch says it's 8
and here comes the moon with her merciless light,
so where is the flash?

No matter how far in we go, how long
we are what we are—
                                        unnatural, human.

# In the Cave

Here, in the mountains where stones prevail,
where the trees squeeze upwards between boulders that move
and the water has no place to go but down,
we have camped in a gap in the cliff, leaving
no messages. We think we are going to survive
here, in the winter that's coming.

You, the adult,
are busy building a defensible cave.
All day I hear your stones falling, dislodged
to fill up old gaps, or open new ones,
to deflect (it is autumn) the coming downfalls
of snow and more stone.

I (the other adult)
inspect my animals, all of them dead,
dismembered and freezing, stores for the winter.
I have also stockpiled descriptions of roots,
and maps for further escapes, and chants
in praise of the winter's radiant snows
(which have yet to descend).

Meanwhile the child we ignore
works in a dark burrow, part of the cave
we can't enter. She says there are monsters in there
who speak with feathers and tongues (we don't listen).
She is busy defacing the walls of her cavern
with spittle and blood

(only her work

will be found).

# What are you doing

What are you doing, trying to push
your way uphill over raw logging cuts,
scrabbling up stream beds, breaking through thickets,
as though it mattered which way you went?
Those are hands not paws growing out of your arms.

Red-faced and huffing, strapped to your shadow like a coolie,
strapped to your ripstop weatherproof pack,
strapped to romantic notions of nature—
which by the way occurred in fields
and meadows, i.e., in civilized lands—
your body connects to a car in a lot, below.

The hawks don't want you out here, they're too ignorant
to beg for your garbage. The bears and the clever
mammals avoid you. The trees are just trees,
they all look alike. The stones have no numbers,
no shapes you remember (but they seem to multiply).
Did you come all this way to gibber with stones?

You don't belong here—did you ever, and where?

What are you proving, importing yourself
and your gear to the wilds? Your daily calories
exceed the environment. What you can gather
is sour, or breaks, and besides you are queasy
about killing.
                    You stop on a ridge and the safe water gurgles
out of your plastic container into your mouth.
In your left pants pocket the keys to the car
are jingling.
                    You can always go back,
you always go back.

# The Observers

The glacier disappoints you:
it resembles (you observe,
through binoculars) not snow
but rather, soiled underwear.

How right you are,
I agree.
            Strange,
how your underwear, discarded
(I later observe)
does not resemble
a glacier at all.

# You don't like the glaciers

You don't like the glaciers we see, they're messy
retreaters; you have tastes and real standards, you prefer
the less obtainable advancers, the clean
blue destruction you expected from glaciers.

Unfortunately all of the locals are shrinking,
getting dirtier each year, their snouts melt off
and the rubble exposed isn't pretty; it's rock
and grey muck and grey dust, even the tarns
and the rapids that come from these glaciers are dirty.

Well we could always come back in a couple millennia
when Xmas card spruces have covered the dirt,
and the *gletschermilch* has been flushed from the waters,

or wait for another Ice Age
to unify shapes, clean up the scene.

Why can't you take Nature as offered?
Shut up and be grateful, you can't afford
your private dynamite, so don't interrupt.

Out on the ice it's our one chance to listen
to whatever the glacier is muttering, to see
how this great swollen hunk and its Neanderthal drains
are ploughing the bedrock. Here we can notice
how accidentally the glacier creates
soil and water, valley and life.

Look, we are mammals, tramping the surface.
The warmth we have
                    is small and not lasting.

# The Dream

In this dream (which is happy)
the canoe I am in lurches (no reason) mid-channel
overturns in a deep dark water  The shore
is so far I don't see it  My gear spills out
like lopsided blossoms, floating and floundering
down to the bottom  I watch it all sink
my notebooks unfinished  3 years irrecoverable
poems visions trivia no one else saw
will see or remember

Now in this dream I am diving (how bravely)
straight down like a loon  I pierce through the water
so swiftly, my feet have somehow grown webs
But the notebooks have opened, the wet pages flutter
away in the darkness, petals or suckers dispersing
I cannot save many, choosing, abandoning
the past to the past

Scrabbling out of the depths (somehow, just barely)
I surface, my 2 hands clutching all the blank pages
dripping, which prove (this is the happiness)
there are poems that will be

# Leaving the Wilderness Campsite

*Boundary Waters*

## 1

A tent-shape of dryness, leaf-duff and roots
cramped by our sleep. A few blond hairs
where a sapling bent back. Imprints of shoes
near the waterline, blurring in mud.
Under the rotted red larch, human
manure. The surrounding lake made smaller
by less than a bucket of water.
Dead branches subtracted, burnt for our comfort
to charwood and ash.
                                        Such traces we leave.

## 2

What are *they* saying, the inhabitants
of thicket and pathway, fur and wing,
about us? What thinking, what smelling,
now we are gone?
                                Are they grateful
for their own kind of silence reopened,
their own kind of gathering and fear?

Or, are they scavengers lured to prefer
more garbage to gorge on, more of the glittering
shards and crumpled grease-smelling foil
we picked from the fire grate?

How could we know?—we who translate
flickerings into data and myth,
creature and species—
                                        in the wilds *they* inhabit
do our questions trail out, breath among leaves?

## 3

Bright ripples, bright metal, the flanks of the canoe
lift from the land shade riding the shallows,
swing out into open lake, our ripples
blur and slide over. Behind us the unanswering
forest heals shut.

## The Man

See, a small space in the woods,
green overgrown with green,
shadows trees brush entangled
At the edge of the clearing a man,
a white man, middle-aged, aging
just his face stands out in the dimness
"dominion over every living thing"
a hunter's jacket, hunter's cap
He lifts the spear of his rifle barrel
aims
with cold, hard, arthritic hands
16 years on the line, finally made foreman,
finally inspector, finally retired
The cold, square, aging jaws of the man
are barely flushed, a tingle of fear
or pleasure as he aims

diagonally across the clearing
into the black furry mass of the bear
She sits on her haunches, back to a stump,
an ancient, massive, dog-nosed brute
pawing the dogs
who yap and skitter away
(My mother's mother, huge in her dress,
sits in the creek, swatting the water and laughing)
She is warm, stupid; she smells of bear
an abundance of flesh, stumpy limbs
stone of a head and little pig eyes
teats where she rears, in the black close fur
She smells like my mother/my mother's mother
she does not understand
she won't get away

The man with the rifle aiming
confers with the other shadowy men
ranging the edge of the clearing
Each in position: they have agreed
which one will have her/whose turn it is
One of them covers the kill

My mother does not understand
rears, paws, shakes her head and its wattles of fur
thinking she's won

Afterwards the body is hoisted
"a sack full of lard" on inaccurate scales
is hung, dressed, weighed on accurate scales
The skull (unshattered, unhurt) is found eligible
for Boone and Crockett official measuring
The head is stuffed and mounted
                                                            safe on the walls
where every evening he enters, approaches
fires recoils fires into the small stupid eyes
"the thrill of a lifetime" my mother

# The Trees in the Peaceable Meadow

A steady rumble    of water sliding
sideways and down    in gorges below
Trickles of water    swelling the limestone
sediments floating    shales giving way
The water's tendrils    probing at bedrock

What has that got to do with us,
ask the trees    in the peaceable meadow
over the gorge
                        We have grown accustomed
to the rumble of water    adjacent, below us
to the plenteous soil    in the craw of our roots
to the unmoving strata    of stone below us
stone going down    to a center of stone

We have never feared water
                                    We have heard of changes
dissatisfied waters    in other valleys
probing, uprooting    original faults
of spruce undercut    and high firs wrenched
from their sockets    into a suddenly opening depth

But how many channels    are actually cut,
out of all the meadows    there be?

And, if this rumbling and scrabbling of water
did concern us,    well, what could we do,
till it happened?
                          (Besides, even if trouble is coming
under our strata,    it may not come
in our time)
                        say the trees in the peaceable meadow

who are founded more surely    than any creature
upon the plates    of the floating earth

# The Table

It was a place where board-lengths do not exist,
where corners and walls do not exist,
a place where all angles gape stupidly open.
Wave piles upon wave, slippery, shifting,
too quick for the eye. The sand grains twist
their uncountable facets, the better to dazzle you.
At the edge of the dunes, driftwood and live wood
entangle, warping and blooming and rasping,
while their buried members subside in the sand.

Alone in this wilderness, I found a table,
full-scale, intact (having ridden what storms?),
washed up and laid on its side. Its squared
oak planks stood up like a target, rebutting
the amorphous winds. Its right-angled legs
held straight in the sand. In all that waste
it was the only made thing. I admired it, and knelt
to haul it upright on its own 4 legs,
like a table. I wanted the years to respect it,
the beetles and weeds to take shelter beneath.
It could say to the wilderness, Here is something not yours,
something still here and not broken.

But when I tried to lift it, by the bottommost edge,
the slanted oak planks shot apart in my hands,
dropped down, guillotines all, on my shins.
I couldn't gather a surface together.
So I left it there, its framework empty
and braces exposed, its planks splayed out
all ways, like slats on a ruined coop.
The small waves chuckled beside me, and the dune weeds
sighed at my back.
                                        Aristotle was right
(and my shins are learning): a thing is its usage:
and a table that is through with being a table
is not a table at all.

# In the Absence of Humans

In the absence of humans, things change,
slowly. A kind of growth,
a readying for growth, sets in.
The stones of the fire circle,
three days behind us, abandoned,
drift heavily open. New bracken
invades our footholds. The land
rebounds. Where our bodies were
the waters heal over, no traces.

Meanwhile, in the city we left,
nature keeps trying, somehow.
Rain flushes the air, industrial
soot settles sideways and down
along with the pigeons, used papers,
used leaves, coughs and debris
and the rest of the cosmic dust.
The paved earth thickens, getting ready
for roots, for rain and decay.

Where the granite began, two hours
behind us, the snake slides back
and sleeps on the trail. In the lens
of your compass, lost among boulders,
moisture like root hairs gathers.
Over our tracks the spider webs
close. The air closes over,
your shout and the sound of your falling
belong to the leaves, no echo.

In the rooms we left, new strata
silt over the untended levels.
Our implements clog, my notebooks
revert to gibberish. Memories
break loose from the artifacts. Our fingerprints
drift. Crevices widen,
the foundation shifts and trickles
towards old burrows. In the earth,
in the air, spores swell, pouring in.

Noon, and we halt on some beach,
not clear on the map. Three ridges
of boulders, still moving, no cedar.
Around us the land rebounds
from the last glacial age. Skinned bears,
we swim among stones. Words float
out of my head, my mouth
garbles your name, I'm losing
my fear, we begin to belong.

# Another Untitled Love Poem

What mammal are you, what whale
blowing and rising
what creature or drifter
washed up on what shore
In the darkness of bodies you
are the hollows and slopes
the ridges of land
and the slippery seas
the heavy invisible planet
pulling my senses
The fleece of your belly and legs
is tangled, alive
an undergrowth rippling
on a strange warm earth
In this harboring darkness
we jostle like swimmers or hulls
swung round in what waters
like waters moving
against and into each other
Your body
is a place unfathomed
a headland emerging
from darkness
My muscles are barriers
are channels
sliding toward you
pulsing and sliding
Wait, the boundaries are changing
The skins
which held us
separate/give way
We float

two creatures sensed
in a ponderous darkness
whose darkness or place
I have always/
will never remember

You emerge into sleep
I watch, drifting off
Your body is yours
a vessel on course
an open, familiar shore
I need not discover

# Equivalencies

The fear of not writing, of having no words,

is the muscles not working, the pack top-heavy,
the hard slime on ledges where the ankle gives way

is the sledge hammer current at the bottom of waves
coming too fast and the swimmer unable

is the baby hung up in the birth canal,
the contractions building but its heartbeat stalls

is the hemorrhage of vision with nothing made yours,
is the flicker of brainwaves in the same stuck dream.

The writing is easy, the having is easy,

is the meadows opening, is the blesséd deep breath
in the mouth of the runner, is the long easy strides

riding and passing the crests of the earth,
is the surge of delivery, the new being riding

the pulsing red channel, is the mountains riding
the slower upheavals of strata and drift,

is the white surge riding the hull of the seed
as it breaks into life, the shapes spilling over

and the words coming through, the deep dream opening
and the words coming true, the words
coming through.

# Packing In With a Man

I had thought I would need him
love under stars
my fellow explorer
Packing into the badlands
following the earth
my needs were quite different

Where the hollows of foothills
opened their silence
he kept asking questions
Where the shoulders of cliffs
trusted our shadows
he plotted with maps
Wherever we went
he needed escapes
to the road and the car
to the money he trusted

When the nighthawk attacked
he timed its return
When the bright quartz signalled
he broke it for samples
In the high arroyos
his bootprints trampled
the fingers of cedar
the prints of the bones

He refused to follow
cloud furrows, wind furrows,
the buried windings
of water and silt,
the dirt track remembered
in a dream of creatures

I couldn't believe
enough for us both
So I took what I needed
Less shelter, more fear

# Untitled Stone Poem

## I

There are places where the earth's cliffs stumble and break,
where the boulders have gathered and the sea waves abide,
places where stone clambers on stone,
skull-shape and slab, tumbling and mauling.

There the animals retreat and go inland for water.
There the humans retreat, no harbor, no paths.
The grasses retreat, unable to seed
in the moving grey stones. There cedar roots grope,
feeding on stone, cramped and retreating.

What light inhabits these barrens of stone
older than humans, borne across waters
no human beholds? What silence inhabits
these slow-heaving stones, and under that silence
what murmuring, learned from the ridges of water
falling into the land, mounting and falling?

## II

If you had the patience of God you could wait
for the fossils hidden in stone to awaken,
for the scoured hollows of boulders to rise,
for the fractures veining the granite to open
as thistle and flower, creeper and wing.

Or, with the lesser patience of death you could wait
for the breath to subside and the flesh ease back
in the thickening earth, mold among mold,
unspecified shards where the soft bones broke.

Or, while the light on the water wavers
and the grey gelid sea drifts toward winter,

if you wait without speaking, without hours or maps,
the stones will begin to forget you are there.
The cedars will rouse and turn to each other,
frond among frond, gravely embracing.

And the light on the water will gather in fullness,
long barrows of light sliding into your eyes
as the sea slides into the stones and garners
slimecell and bubble, bright furrows of life:

and the stones will speak, stone among stone
and stone among water, in a tongue that is known
to the skin of your eyes, a breath remembered
in the pit of your breath, a hymn of grey stone
that will enter the shining furrows of brain

and never translate into words for the humans.

# The Summer Woman

Sprawled on the mountain's flank, half-hidden
under apple leaves gone wild, she watched
the osprey hover above the cedars,
wheel and glide home. Squinting she saw
the tinfoil gleam of the fish it had carried
from the glittering inlet, miles below.
Closing her eyes to the sun, she felt
the skulls of the nestlings thicken, warm
as an infant's skull under her hand;
she felt her own skull lift in the sun,
the layers of calcium thin out in the steep
bright air.
                    Over the osprey's nest
the fronds of the cedars roused themselves,
stirred and subsided; she waited to feel
her own skin stir, hairs drift, as the invisible
wind descended, riffling the meadow
and its fringes of bracken around her, lifting
the low apple leaves, carrying and losing
the voices of the men she'd borne, husband
and sons, far echoes absorbed by the forest.
Alone with the mountain, she breathed the wind
and the chill it bore from the cedars' darkness;
saw beyond seeing the packed mold shift
in the path they were building, the felled trees twist
out of their lines, the unnameable beetles,
cells, root hairs, devouring their work.
She had done enough.
                              Sleeping or waking,
the brightness slid by. She felt in her head
the mountain moving its haunches toward winter,
the meadow lie cramped under the drifts
of approaching snow, the cedars stiffening

in a brittle air, the talons of ice
clawing their trail and giving it back
to the mountain.
                                        Enough. The warm bracken leaned
its fronds towards her; the meadow retreated,
root by root, from the invading wilderness;
the cedars rejoiced, green among green.
About her the ponderous slope of the mountain
wheeled and fell in its silent arc
away from the sun, bearing her breath
with its burdens, carrying the trace of her warmth
headlong in space, a chip on the surface,
wheeling and falling.

# The Habit of Fire

By the wilderness lake I settle my haunches
in a nest of stones, lean back on a deadfall
carcass of pine, the only shelter,
cold but not wet. Behind me thickets
waiting for nightfall; no openings my size,
no one's been here. The sun slides down
over the green-black cones of the mountains
rimming the lake; the sky flares up
like a mirror, pearl on the water, glaring
and greying. Suddenly thinned air, like water,
wraiths of cold swimming towards me;
too late to wash up. Grey fire stones and kindling
readied before me, unlit; deadfall
enough for hours.
                                Black mountains, black sky;
stone shapes changing. I see through a face net
my personal aura of insects close in,
signalled by warmth. Things crackling and listening
behind me; the sky goes *Whooee, Whooee,*
no one I know.
                        Smell of horses
from somewhere, then gone; no horses out here,
anything that big is probably bear.
New prints today on the logging road,
in the place where I backtracked for water, bear crossing
over the prints of my Vibram soles,
full-grown. While I yawn, the road I will follow
leans downhill, gullies, lets go; stones topple;
thickets I broke are healing behind me.
I don't want to know how the blackness spreads
under my ribs.
                        If I died out here
it would be my doing, not theirs; I smell

of textiles and fire; even dead they'd avoid me.
I couldn't live here.
                              In the blackness a lapping
of water or muzzle; the air says something,
gibberish or warning, and quits when I move,
matches in hand, to strike open the fire
that stops me from seeing.

# After the Surveyor's Death

# My Father Is Diving

My father is diving, my father who does not swim
plunges down through a glittering rectangle of water;
ticklish bubbles of sun trail at his heels,
in the moving web of light at the bottom he turns,
jackknifes, and rises, flinging his forelock
like a flop-eared spaniel. When he stands on earth
the water slides over his body like summer, like sun;
before I can praise him he dives and he rises again,
spouting the water, in this summer that never occurred
for my father who does not swim
(in snapshots he stands at the edge of the boardwalk,
heavy of foot, heavy of mouth,
eyeing the sea and finding her shifty):
for my father who has just gone under the surgeon's knife
and who will emerge upright in a spinal brace
I remember this swimming day
and my father, who is old, is young.

# After the Surveyor's Death

### I: Arrangements

When the man left,
his medicines waited by his place at the table,
a group of dark bottles labelled for refills,
casting small shadows.

When the man left,
neighbors brought cakes: chocolate, his favorite,
applesauce, which he tolerated, and spice, and lemon,
and two carrot cakes with healthfood frosting,
which he would have distrusted.

When the man left,
the voice of his son grew sterner, like his;
the bowels of his son went sour, like his;
his son's back slumped, and his heavy silences
settled among them.

When the man left,
the picture nearest to smiling was moved
to the living room console, facing the visitors,
between his ashtray and the incoming flowers,
on display, and his wife stood beside it, stranded
among neighbors and kindred.

### II: Permutations

When the man left,
the scores of his solitaire games, recorded
on packets of paper saved from the office,
lay stacked on his desk, next to the stacks
of unscored paper, thousands and thousands
of chances played out in hours of retirement,
where he turned his back to the light and the chatter,

his head to the wall, permuting the numbers,
his witness, his work.

When the man left,
a lumpy old man, older than he,
and happier, and poorer, walked in the darkness,
wheezing and slow, smiling at strangers,
shepherding his mutts, mother and whelp,
sagging and yelping, up the steep dead end
of the street by the graveyard.

### III: Effects

When the man left,
no storm flared forth from the sun, no god
bargained with death, no season trembled
nor stone took notice: no bird failed to soar,
nor weed to blossom: the earth kept turning,
and no number was broken.

When the man left,
weeks followed weeks, and the living kept living;
there was only, in the hearts of the next of kin,
a kind of thickening or scar, a deposit,
as of sediment laid down.

When the man left,
the earth he'd surveyed kept slipping, distorting
the heights he had fixed; the faults of the continents
tugged at his benchmarks, undermining his stations;
the grid of his distances shrivelled and bellied
beyond dominion.
He would have approved,
he would have welcomed all drift and creation,
new work for his numbers.

## Photograph Taken at My Father's House

This is his house. In the foreground the grandchild
holds up a mallet, the blue one he gave her,
and waves with her gap-toothed smile for someone,
it must be the neighbor. We are all too busy
to play her croquet. She has his cowlick,
his reddish-brown hair. In the background the road
lies empty, a white curve of glare
between lots. Over the top of the picture
Atlantic clouds are floating, endlessly
beautiful white out of beautiful blue,
safe as the developers promised, beyond cities
and winter. Behind the child is the long
screened porch with the blue-webbed chairs
where he sat beside Mother, helping the sun rise,
they said, where my brother with nothing to say
will sit tonight.
                    Now, out of range,
my brother is shovelling flowers and peelings
into the compost which is next to the garden
no one will want. These are the flowers
from someone's wedding, glads and white iris,
the ladies from church brought them over, to help.
Flowers do not last in this heat. At the florist's
they told us, *Buy mums, Mums are the best*
*to stand up in this heat,* and we dutifully bought
all of their mums, from us and the others
who could not attend. I am out of the picture,
hosing the garden and the struggling geraniums
Mother forgot, hosing the yard
and the driveway for guests. I have tried all morning
but the water sinks down through green-brown grass
and is gone in the sand. Plants have to thicken

to stand it down here, even the gaudiest
live with drought at their roots.
                                        Soon we are going
where the mums have been sent, to a shading canopy
on a wide bright hill. And after the ceremony,
the words and the silence, the flowers will be left
in the square of shade, and the director's son,
correct in black, will lead Mother out,
holding her elbow to be sure she keeps going.
And she in her dress of not quite black,
not quite correct, will leave him abruptly,
walking too fast, not looking at us
on the long ride back, she didn't expect
to be left so quickly in the house of the photograph
where we will try to help, answering the doorbell,
thanking the guests who are trying to help.

# In the Year of Your Death

In the year of your death I drove North
alone, with only the child that was there,
no new one inside me. Road drifts and darkness,
coming in too late to the wilderness cabin—
the bay iced over, the track through the woods
ice over mud over ice, the low car
slewing in ruts, no place to stop—
why was I there?
                                        In the year of your death,
at the northernmost spine of land before water,
the old trail to the point flooded over, half-ice,
not safe with the child. In the bowl of cedar
between bay ice and marsh, where no one could see,
the animal's skeleton, headless, brass casings
beside it, around us the silence. The child
gathered the pelvis and blades of its shoulders,
made masks for her face till I stopped her
    *touching your face at the viewing,*
    *Why is he painted like that?*
I didn't say why.
                                        In the rented cabin
the skull on a shelf, a candle inside,
souvenir from the hunters or gatherers before us.
The woodpile wet ice and wet pulp, I couldn't
stop shivering, in thermals, in down; the bad tooth
broke off in my mouth. Deer tracks by the pump,
ice shouldering old ice out in the bay,
why was I there?
                                        Packing out to the car,
the child balked in the drifts, I panicked
and had to keep going, I didn't know why,
there was nothing but silence.

# The Traveller

You would have come by car, the old
squared grey sedan, the back way past
the unploughed field, slowing, turning
up the steep dark slope beside the garden
of my first owned home: I was kneeling, pulling
last year's weeds from clay, when I heard
your car and saw its grey, the driver's
window open and your elbow out,
your blue shirt fading out in greys,
light on your glasses, glinting, white,
your almost-smile: I saw you there,
that was the way you would have come.

# Inheritance

*Did you not father me?*

Father, I am not your son.
Though I have your heavy habits
and your heavy bones, your blue straight eyes
whose gaze goes outward from the dark within,
I am not your son.
Though I sit with half my life lived through
as you sat, slumped, my heavy forehead
clamped to paper reckonings,
my heavy words held back
before the quick and baffling, peopled world,
I am not your son.
Though I see the proud, disordered hills
staked out with measurements your surveys made,
though I wander from your numbered, levelled paths,
though your distance charts my wilderness
in lines you would not recognize,
I am not your son.
Though I seek your faith and do not find,
though I try to hold your straitened righteousness,
and count the doubts that keep the vision off,
though the chill of your despair spreads in my skull,
I am not your son.
Though I live as you did, narrow, good,
steadfast at work, mistrusting play,
longing for the easy, noisy joys,
yet keeping loneliness my closest friend
and silence as my habitat,
I am not your son.
Though I know you did not know why you lived thus,
though your death is one year past and done,
though you are my father still,
yet I am not your son.

## In Praise of the Natural Flowing

Out of the storm pipe, between the old path
and the unsold lots, the water journeys
at will this winter, flowing and floating
over its sheathing of ice: I see the clear riffles
angling and falling seaward; the continents
forming and formed, where ice, mud,
weedstuff and human discards run aground;
the channels and shallows forced between continents;
the reed clumps hummocked and footed like trees
with silt and debris; and down through the water
a fragile mud-tissue holding, half-shielding
the dead mingled leaves and the fragments of weeds,
like wingstuff in amber; the reed stalks prone,
combed out like the hairs of a long-drowned beast;
and the powdery silt and the clear openings in silt
where the water has winnowed its earth: I see
beside the water the gradual shelvings
of ice, contoured like land, reaching out
from its shorings and ending; and over the still places
the frail film ice, transparent as cirrus
or the membranes which form over the unborn:

I see in this world the natural flowing,
older than Genesis, slower than clouds
but faster than stone, which forms the rivers,
the lowlands and channels and continents of earth:
which feeds on life and tends ever towards life:

and I praise it, in gratitude and bitterness, knowing
this flow, vulnerable and beautiful, is permitted
to be this winter, between the worn path
and the scrawny stakes with the flapping red plastic
which claim this world.

# Human Love Poem

Sun wakes us, and the squirrels yell
from ice-slick trees. You stroke my breast,
I curl around your newborn warmth
and give you milk. Small skull, small foot,
we share the river of your thirst,
the blood-warmed slope you burrow in,
the breathing murmurs and the pulse
that drifts into your feeding sleep.

Outside, beyond your dreaming hands,
tree shadows vein the ice-bound roofs.
Raccoons break elder buds, or fight
for bread I left beneath the tree;
their young go hungry, cold, go nowhere
in our subdivided world.
Is it the fit survive? My species'
cunning and its luxuries
prevail: therefore in helpless trust

you nuzzle, suckling, predator
as I am predator, the fierce
inheritors of earth: therefore
I do what any creature would:
I turn to you, and feed my young.

# The Inheritor

September, and these cold hill streets where the Quakers
failed and died out. Beside the old road
spirea goes grey, goes bald, and the tame
barberry argues with gusts, claws
at the cold, useless as grief. Overgrown,
dying back, ivy billows and tugs
at old mortar, old walls. High overhead
blue sheetwinds of cold race for the South,
for the warmth, for the glaring great hill of sand
where my father lies dead and dead indeed
under heaven. Here shelter draws into itself,
crumbles like mortar. Here the great burial hill
pulls down its toothless stones, though the hands
on these soft Quaker tablets point upwards to heaven.
Here memory trails out, useless. Upright
against the cold I push the bundled child
of his bones, child of his eyes, child
of the year of his death. At the crest of the hill
I kneel and hold the bundled child
to warm my hands. Below, the empty
trees, the tame hill streets; the cold
earth falls away. We living build
on hills of sand, on hills of shifting clay.

# The Headstone and the Bearer

*The body bears much that is weary in life,*
*more after death.*

The headstone likes things settled,
surveyed with clear title,
laid out in perpetual symmetry.

Below, the bearer has shuffled
and muddled its chances,
caved in under pressure.

The headstone stands upright,
has a place to uphold,
belongs in the ranks of the prosperous.

The bearer forgot to exercise,
lost track of accounts,
laid down and went under.

The headstone knows its own character,
its cubits of stature,
its history, its dates.

The bearer had bristles and snarls,
aches and ambitions,
and has gone all to pieces by now.

The headstone says what it means,
in granite,
in marble,
in tablets of bronze.

The bearer made many remarks,
worthy or not,
to many a bearer,
none of them lasting.

Under wind, under snow, under God
the headstone
waits for the judgment.

The bearer has suffered and backslid,
deserted all causes,
abandoned the living,
lapsed out of sight.

In the November twilight the headstone ponders
ritual and time,
lily and yew and wrought iron—

and, in league with the other headstones, rises indignant as soap
over vandals and lovers,
erosion and moles,
and ribboned grave blankets with plastic red berries.

Deep in the folds of the earth
the bearer lies idle,
does nothing at all
forever and ever, Amen.

# Fragment

In this dream that is mine
you are in your right body
red veins in your skin
your heavy head lifted
sun on your face
your worn blue shirt
soft at the sleeves, rolled up
your eyes
blue as mine
You are here, you are real
Your face
turns towards me, you are smiling
There is all the time left
We have all the time left in the world

## from ——— *Territories, Here & Elsewhere*

## Pictures Not in Our Albums

Somewhere it is still
a dream of safety, our young
parents hauling us up the dark pass,

Father blocking the wheels of the trailer
while Mother lets go the emergency brake
and eases the Ford into low, pulls forward
and slows, pulls forward and waits.
As if I had watched from a roadcut

I see the small oval Ford
pale in the shadows, our grey-blue trailer
weighing it down, the asphalt road
falling away on all sides into blackness,
the curve ahead climbing to blackness.

Across the vast basin of desert,
the night-drowned ridges and foothills,
a coyote howls and is answered. There are
no lights but ours on the earth,
no farther lights except the slow stars.

In the back of the car, in the warm
nest of children, I drift
from sleep to waking, breath
to breath, as the car labors
and rests, labors and rests,

and the night outside is a slow swelling sea
lapping the mountains, black waters
so vast that a ship could founder,
a thousand lit ships go down,
all lights but our own go under.

## Epithet

The first man I called Sir
the wrong way, not meaning it, was the one
who stopped his black Chevy on the hill
near high school, Could I come over
and show him the route to West
Cherry Lane? I could, he didn't
look dirty or strange, just grown-up
but young, with a dark plaid shirt
and his sleeves turned up, and a road map
unfolded over the steering,
like my father, on trips. I was trying
to see where he pointed, when I couldn't
help seeing his other hand hefting
something below, it looked
alive but somehow skinned over,
like sausage. I knew he wanted
me to think it was really all him.
He wasn't ugly or anything
different, he had a regular nose,
his eyes were dark and real serious,
giving orders somehow. He was handsome
in fact. This was all broad daylight,
and houses I knew, my regular
route. So I called him Sir
and more Sir, pretending I thought
nothing was wrong, while I backed
away from his arm, which had hairs
like the minister's, and the closed car door,
and got back to the papers I'd been folding
on the storm drain corner. His car
drove off up the hill, getting smaller,
like a little black toy. The street
stayed empty. I looked down at my jeans,

which were brand-new from Penney's, with a plaid,
red-and-white, lining the cuffs.

Next day, in the lunchroom, I started
to tell my best friends, at the end
of the table. They giggled a lot,
Was he handsome? Did he ask you to hold it?
Did he show you his money? I wanted
to ask was it really all him,
but didn't know how. Then Agnes,
who was bigger, said he was just a pervert,
they always came out in the spring
back home, why once there was one waiting
at the bus stop, with his fly wide open,
and she and her cousins just laughed
and pointed, till he cussed them out
and ran off in the woods. Just a pervert,
that's all. I felt better, and thirsty
and hungry. Agnes had finished
most of my lunch, which was chowder
with franks, so she gave me her pie,
which was cinnamon apple with topping,
and better than usual. So I had
two desserts, before the bell rang.

# Making Paths

There are always
reasons to turn
aside, or stop
in your tracks: spring
beauty, bloodroot,
the vulnerable jack-
in-the-pulpit crop
up mid-path; mole
works collapse and foxes
leave scats just where
you'd step; at the creek-
crossing log, the trash
boxelders and dead
poplar lean, worse
after rains; going up
the cut bank, spicebush
extends its green
berried fronds, blocking
your progress; not to mention
the assorted thorn-
berry stems, the young
strangler vines, the deep
glossy leaflets invading,
or the fertile hitch-
hiking ticks.
                    Obviously
nature prefers
you not to come
this way, or any
way here. You can argue
that deer trample anything,
weather has always
cut swaths, fungus

downs oaks, even the field
mice gnaw tunnels
all over their fields:
aren't your muscles
and sweat entitled
to territory?
                    Still
it doesn't seem fair,
making the earth
say paths, your right
arm hooked onto metal,
slashing and flailing
through second-growth woods
that have only illiterate
roots and swelling green
life to oppose you.

# Accident, 1946

Like erosion, memory
selects the shards
that turn up: the trooper
leaning one boot
on the shiny chrome ball
of our car's trailer hitch
squints and says *Buster,*
*do you know how lucky*
*you are? This little Ford*
*would've flipped right over,*
*kiddies and all, if*
*you'd had safety*
*chains when that house trailer*
*broke loose. But the law*
*is the law in Kentucky,*
*I have to write you*
*a ticket, see? Nah,*
says the second trooper,
*chains wouldda held,*
*you wouldn't a lost her*
*at all.* Then my father
who is still the tallest
man there, who surveys
and maps the whole country,
just stands there, hands hanging,
like a kid lined up for recess
first day at a new school.
Was it a joke or for real
when one of them said
he ought to get fired
for breaking the law?
I remember it was safer
not asking if fired

was real fire. Then afterwards
there was only my family,
my mother driving, though it wasn't
her turn, and my father
beet-red down his neck,
as we followed the truck
that was towing our tilted home
with its bashed-in end—
how it whipped back and forth,
crossing the center line,
and the doll clothes that were caught
in the hole under my bed
flapped and spilled out on the highway,
going past like a movie
we watched without talking—
scraps, outfits, even
the pink Sunday dress
where I'd sewed a sleeve shut
for my one-armed doll.

# Hallway

I have opened their door
at the wrong time and he's walking
towards me to shut it,
barefoot, full frontal,
a word that I didn't
know then.
                    His face
where I am trying to look
is maybe more red
or in shade. It's the tightness
of his eyes and his mouth
I remember.
                    She lies flat
on their bed, her arms
at her sides like a clothespin
you could dress as a stopper-
head doll.
                    Their curtains
were closed, and I
was the only one talking.

# Stories Waiting to Happen

*Kingman, Arizona, 1948*

It's Stage Robbers Gulch, I take
the high ledge, guarding my sister,
as the eastbound train with its blazing light
breaks free from the valley's dark ridge
and charges towards us. The pounding rumble
builds to a roar like stampedes,
Hercules squirms and yips
inside my rodeo shirt. Now it's thunder
all through us, the engine and coal car
breathing black fire. Boxcars, ore cars,
flatcars clanking and swaying
below, *22, 23,* when I squint
their tops flow together like a snake's
flat back, moving fast over sand.
*44, 55, 66,* the roaring
rises and falls, *104, 105,*
*You're not the shortest, not*
*the longest, you're the loudest,*
*we're the strongest.* Then the caboose
trailing lights, and the men waving back
when they see us up high, waving
our cowboy bandannas.
Sometimes after school
a long train will be stopped, so long
we can't see the end. Rio Grande, Pacific,
Topeka, Santa Fe, we cross the great shadows,
watching for trainmen, keeping clear
of the couplings and track. Hercules teethes
on his leash—could he smell out a tramp
in a boxcar? We know the scare stories,
tramps sliced in two, the fugitive
riding the rods under cars
who got bumped by a switch, the two kids
caught on a one-track trestle—

the smart one lay flat between rails,
eyes closed, and was saved as the train
thundered over, but his friend tried
to outrun it and failed.
                    One day I climb
the steep bolted ladder, hand over hand
to the roof of a boxcar—Colorado,
sealed shut. Bending low like a scout,
clutching the grab iron on top, I can't see
where the stopped train ends—I want
to go striding from roof to roof, arms out
like a hero.
          My sister waits, holding tight
to Hercules below—does she see
I'm afraid to stand up? These trains
take forever to get any speed—could I ride
to the sand wash, jump free? The train
humps itself together, couplings clash
and reclash, the boxcar under me
lurches hard forward, I scramble
down the ladder like a comic-strip coward,
drop off and run. At least there weren't
any boys, at least my sister
won't tell.
          Years later, a boy
who was first board in my high school chess
will hitch a ride on a slow night freight.
At the crossroads his two friends jump
and roll clear, but he slips between cars,
the wheels slice his leg at the thigh,
he bleeds to death while they run
for help.
          I only danced with him once—
were his eyes blue or brown? In memory
my sister squints up, scared of the boxcars
but ready to do what I said,
stay back or climb on.

## Crossing, 1963

*Kumasi to Bolgatanga, Ghana*

A clear day, a clear stretch
on the two-lane road going north
through dry open bush:
                                        then the crest
of that nameless hill where I swerve
to the free lane to get past the men
crammed in an open-back lorry
stopped in the road; they sit watching
as I clear them by less than a hand.
From nowhere
                          a man on a bicycle
cuts across the free lane, ten,
twelve feet between us, I can't slow
fast enough, can't swerve into the men
or out to the edge where he'll be
if he makes it. Now he sees,
his mouth falls open, his hand
slants up from the handlebar, palm out
as if to say *Stop* or push back
the car. I see the bike stall,
then the slow jackknifing tilt
of front wheel and frame
                                        doesn't happen,
his torso stays upright, the bike
lifts into balance as if
hauled up from the sky, he clamps
his hands to the bars, he pedals
or maybe coasts free, the bike
stays upright and he clears the edge
of my windshield, he's clear,
saving us both.

I can still see
the blue lorry, the men in their head rags
peering out like sightseers, the thin
trader boy wedged between bundles,
waving me on.
I can partly see
the man on the bike, his white shirt
and wide-legged shorts, the clothes
of a man with some schooling or work
in the city. He was solid and big-boned
for a Ghanaian; he'd had enough food
as a child. The bicycle too,
with its once-red paint, was progress,
ambition.
Perhaps he went south
as a teacher, a minor official,
a clerk; then retired well-off
in his village. Perhaps he still sees
in his head the bright flash of that day
when we held to our paths, not knowing
but sparing each other.

## Territory

If you didn't need sleep
and comfort and warmth, you wouldn't
take space like you do
                    This corner
for instance, sheltered, well-lit,
on a safe enough street where nice
people pass
            If you didn't need safety
you wouldn't be here, hunched
by the stairwell, head in your arms
like a traveller braced for a crash,
your soft parts covered, your dead
weight propped on the bags that are home

If you made us feel good, if you looked
like us, you could stay

## Interrogation

*National Airport, 1989*

There is a man whose job it is
to have an ordinary look
about his face, an ordinary
suit and way of standing back,
almost at ease, like someone
sidelined from the airport queues,
his eyes rescanning semblances
as if to pass the time, his hands
kept free, his task a random-seeming
beckoning and bending close
to ask:
        *When did you pack your bags?*
*Have they been in your control since then?*
*Was there anyone who gave you anything*
*to carry on this flight?*
                                In these good times,
in better terminals, we need
such welcomings.

## Preparation

I do
what I would have done
had a different call
come through: get up
too early in the silent
house, and kneeling
on the green old-gardener's pad
you gave me, crumple
news to fill the fire-
place grate, two even rows
laid straight across,
then scrapwood from our plenteous
falling oaks; make sure
there's some odd bumpy
piece used up, no green
or questionables; start
six good flarings from the one
struck match.
                    The black
outside our window
greys. The hunting cat
wants in. A truck
shifts down to climb
some farther hill.
                    The first
flames waver from the wood
and partly hold. I use
my breath to make
the weak ones catch,
then feed a splinter
to the light. The orange
warmth spreads. I place
two heavy lengths

you've split and hauled
up our clay hill, along
my salvaged wood-
chip paths; then stretch
out on the camper's mat
we shared that one
long night. The fed
cat circles near to bask
beside me in this wordless
time where wood becomes
its pulsing chaos
flow.
        Five hours
from now, you might
still want this sort
of fire.
          Meanwhile,
I tend our long-spared
hearth, as I would need
to do, had the second
engine on that foreign
plane lost power, and
that early waking call
not come from you.

## Love Poem, Later

What I would give you now
is that night in the open
you wanted, the one free summer
we drove west through the Badlands:
we would climb that wind-stripped
summit, and lie quietly down,
sheltering each other
while darkness flooded
all chasms and strata below,
the last light gathered
on our one pale island,
and stars arced slowly
past our waking and sleeping.

When I rouse you now,
after so many years
of wishbones and plenty,
it could be the same stars,
though lessened or lost
in these piedmont skies;
out past the hammock
there is some such darkness
welling up from the creek
to our walls: see, in this late
summer haze, how the moon's shafts
reach through the boundary pines
as never before in our lives,
refracting bright motes
from all the world's burning.

# Afterwards

# Odds

It is true that those who push the weak ones aside
to get to the lifeboat/the ammo/the grub—
who marooned on an island of ice
lie in their tents, nursing their grudges,
threatening and filching while others provide—
may live to be rescued, beget, and die in warm beds.

And those who are lost early on, without issue, stay dead.

And those who go out on the floes or the edge of the cliff
to bring back the eggs/the hatchlings/the seal meat for all,
who when birds and mammals have left
and no ship appeared, make soup from skins and offal,
and share it out fairly, so all may live—

even those who secretly give scraps of their own
to the sick and the hungry-eyed young
may live to be rescued, raise children, and die in warm beds.

Can we ask evolution, or whatever god
is calling these shots:
Why are you stacking the deck for both sides?
Are goodness and greed equally fit to survive?
Or would you rather, after that fuss
in the garden, keep the big-headed creatures like us
from fixing the odds?

## When Towers Burn

Should smoke refuse to rise, or drift?
Should the whorling, windswept earth stand still?
Should time slip back, and thousands live
where ashes blazed and towers fell?

Fire of safety, shelter, light;
fire of magma, terror, war:
how many cities torched the sky
before these burning pillars soared?
How many thousand lives fed flames
before our histories began?

The man necklaced with a burning tire:
the fleeing child, her skin on fire:
the men consumed who flew those planes
like burning spears into the towers
that rose and flamed and fell as ash:
these images replay, endure.

Letters and flowers for the lost
surround a pit of smoldering grey.
We breathe the embers and the dust
of those who found their stairwells flame
and those who raced the flames to save
till stairs and floors plunged down through flame.

Smoke takes its ancient, coiling shapes,
divides like clouds, drifts out like spores
to seed the swollen whorls of sleep,
the waking chaos blooms of war.

# Barrier Island, Assateague Refuge

*14 September 2001*

## 1

Love, what are we given,
what can we keep?

This open-mouthed island rising from sea:
this multitudinous flowing of grains
that will rise for no baker's kneading—
                                                            quartz
feldspar magnetite shellshard spilling
light from our hands to the wind:
                                                    these waves
of air-borne sand smoothing our paths:
these waves of sea-spume climbing and falling
over our tracks, the petroglyph tracks
of sandpipers feeding, the oozing bubbles
of mouths hidden in sand, all seeking
flotsam set free in the ancient seethe.

Here the great plates caught, the new earth quickened
with creeper and vine, birdcall and breath.

Here storms peel open the dunes, flints
and shell heaps spill forth, scars from the fires
of those before us, shadows in sand.

## 2

What can I give you, here where the shallow
barrier of beach rolls over, where the hook
of the cove closes and fills? Here where the marsh
that was gathered and speared, grazed and channeled
subsides into peat that the storms pull under,
heave back into land?

Here our sheltered bodies
roll over in sleep, seeking what shorelines
and handholds, our synapses riding what surges
into that seafoam of light, rebounding
light into light—
as in the chambered eye
of the Fresnel lens whose light once flashed
from a shoreline, a town washed inland and gone.

These days in the absence of contrails, the grounding
of planes, sun floats as before, clouds
gather their harboring darkness as if
no fiery towers had soared on our screens,
no dust from their falling entered these skies.

### 3

Spared for a time we are glimmers, hooked
and freed in the tumbling thresholds of sand:

though I would give you these days without end, would make
this clasping new and forever—
salt
in your beard, your weathering body on mine,
the sand-grained tributaries of your hand—

oh love, we roll and spill through time,
bright grains set free, flung in the nets
where green becomes new green, new pulsing
chambered blood.
Lost cries, torn waterweed
the island heaps and spills, bright grains
commingling with the sand-blast wind,
the live and rampant, crowning sea.

## Report from an Alien Planet

We have found the canals that could be geometry,
geology, chance. We have found the water
in ice fog and rock, the water and air
locked in the white polar caps, the traces
of breathable oxygen. Suited like divers,
we have probed dark craters for meteors bearing
the compounds of life, for stones that could
have fallen from cairns, for pockets of oxide
that could have been tools. Tethered to lifelines,
we have measured vast shapes in the wind-scoured cliffs
that could have been human, or life-form, or god.

We came hoping for seeds and fibers, cisterns
and dams. For mineworks, hieroglyphs, ruins.
For messages, warnings, from those who built
canals unswerving from pole to equator
while earth life drifted in froth and slime.
We hoped to find burials, or bones untended,
the great rib cages of beings like us
who evolved and perished in the thinning air.

We can stay no longer. We have planted our sensors
on promising slopes, transmitted our claims,
secured our last samples for the long flight back.
Our mothership hangs in the airless depths,
our home planet floats like a blue-green moon
whose sheltering air will be our last barrier.

We will speak, if we return, of data
harvested, materials tested, voyages
charting our cosmos; of seeing more deeply
into the dark implosions of matter,
the primordial light spark, the silence of god.
Whatever we say to urge a return
will be used to replace us with alien metals,
equations, breathless all-seeing machines
evolved to transmit without hunger or dreams.

# Exodus

They carry a world in their eyes. In their bodies
history takes shelter, a cyst in the gut, a living
blossom embedded in brain.
                                        Pear trees, apricots,
their blossoms uncounted, on fire. The marriage
photos, the marriage bed, birth beds,
deathbeds, on fire. Roofs and outbuildings,
animals and fields, windows and doorways,
on fire.
        Shots, orders, fire.
The winnowing of men, herded like beasts
to the harvest. *But my father's beasts*
*were not beaten, not shot as they ran, not slashed*
*again and again.*
                                Shots, screams, silence.
*Then we heard laughter, the joyous triumphant*
*laughter* of those who came that night
with weapons and masks, with armor
and laughter. *Yet some of us knew*
*voices among them, the man who drove*
*the late bus, the boy from the baker's stall*
*who counted our coins.*

* * *

The hundreds, the thousands,
the hundreds of thousands, shapes of dust
on the roads.
                        The rain, the thirst,
the cold. The dazed man without shoes,
the red-brown mud caked on his socks.
The father's father, his face caved in,
his tooth glass knocked to the floor as he fled.

The children who do not look up,
the children who look without seeing.

The slow ones with only their slippers,
the ones who are carried or dragged,
the ones who must not be lost.

* * *

In the days, the winnowing of women,
the young ones who do not come back.
The two who came back, rivulets of blood
on their feet. The shame of those who saw
their bent heads.
                                        The woman in black
holding her belly. The woman who dropped
at the side of the road, emptying the child
from her belly.
                                    *Sometimes there was bread, hidden*
*or given.* Water wherever, the flushed cheeks
and blank eyes of the children, the worn
animal faces of women holding the hands
of children.
                              The women down on their knees,
scooping the ditchwater, streamwater, snow.
The women tending the children
in darkness, sharing a basin of water,
*look, stars you can drink.*

* * *

She says *there were twelve in her family, before.*
Tonight they are counted as nine

of those who are lucky, they have reached
the dark field of a country where oranges
and bottles of water, blankets and bread
will be given.
                                        Stars she can name
bloom through the clouds, hunter
and prey.
                          Shots, orders, fire
at her daughter's home where she lived.
Shots, orders, fire at her brother's house
where she fled.
                                        In her arms she cradles
the drowsing child of her second daughter,
the one who stares and won't speak.

Roads, paths, woods,
roads. Her toe has turned black.
She says *it is hard to walk up a mountain.*

Note: Ajete Bulig, 65, is the poem's last speaker; see David Finkel, "Exodus," *Washington Post,* 19 April 1999, C1, C4.

# Pond, Late Summer

Where herons once fished, rafts of algae
drift like false green islands riding
the silt-laden waters. Somewhere upstream
construction blooms. Here the wood duck glides
with her brood of nine, male and female now
revealed in crests or white-ringed eyes;
their grazing paths meander through green
like silica in marble.
                                        Then a V of ripples,
the low rafts heave on their swollen sea,
a young muskrat surfaces, shakes water, dives
as we count, one thousand and six, then rises
in the shallows beside us to dabble its gleanings.
Past the ducklings another furred stone goes under,
rises and splashes, then heads for the first—
we see its back gleam, its arched tail swing
like a rudder as it swims the strait they have cut
through land-shapes of drifting green slurry.
The first does not flee, they nuzzle like wolf-cubs,
then dabble their harvest.
                                                  We watch their tiny
rat feet lifting weeds, their small faces munching.
I want to give thanks for their trust. Around us
the pond is a breathing sea at rest:
if I were to kneel and slide my hands
into that living water, I would drift
like a stick in that warm green lapping,
like a ripple, lifted and freed.

## Afterwards, You Learn

Afterwards, you learn to say
you were lucky, the last-year's cubs
stayed safely behind her, breaking
the thickets for berries. Lucky
the wind from the darkening valley
turned cold, and your jacket was heavy,
and zipped to the neck. Lucky
you knew, too late for retreat
in that clearing of downfall and stone,
to drop and go fetal, arm
over neck, playing dead. Lucky
the backpack came off like an arm,
saving most of your arm, and kept her
busy till the grunting cubs
called her back to their feast.

Afterwards you learn to say
that the fault was yours: you were tired,
you were stubborn, making up for lost time
on that summer-growth trail through clearings
and thickets, the wind in your face,
not bothering to sing out or warn
what was there besides you, not waiting
for warnings to reach you.

But sometimes, in sleep, you go back
to that stonefall clearing, that edge
of safety where your scalp hair rises
like hackles for no reason you see,
and there is still enough time to go back
as that dark shape lifts upright
from its tangle of shadow, like a man
in a burly fur suit, peering out,
and you wake with the ghost hairs rising
like fur on your unscarred neck
and perfect right arm.

# An Old Story

Now, in our time, he is safe
in a chamber built in his honor.
The most skillful attendants, precautions,
care no Pharaoh could buy.
Now he is valued by nations,
recorded in history. Now
we have nations and history.

At the end, caught by snow on the high
mountain ridge, he fell or lay down
in a bowl in the rock, his head
pillowed on rock, his ear
folded under. He lay sideways, protecting
the ribs that were broken weeks before.
At the last his fingers let go
of the ember carrier, a birch-bark tube
that rested nearby. For five thousand years
the snows kept him safe.

Now we inherit his goods: tools,
pannier, fire pouch, the healing fungus.
Scraps of the thatched grass cloak.
Fur clothing, skillfully sewn.
Axe of copper and yew, dagger
of flint and ash. His two arrows
broken, the fur quiver damaged,
days or weeks before the high ridge.
His old bow gone, the bow string saved.
Gnawed splinters of bone, from dried ibex meat.
A sloe, that ripens in autumn. Husks
of einkorn and wheat in the ember carrier,
remnants of threshing.

An able man in his forties,
our experts say: a hunter or herdsman
come home to his village, then forced to flee
and keep going, wounded, ill-armed,
at a dangerous season.

We inherit his story, and shape it
with ours. We do not want
to think him a fool, or crazed.
Give us Cain, give us Abel,
an impossible task, a struggle,
a judgment. Or a village slaughtered,
and he alone escaped.

We know he could not go back.

We know he had hope. He had almost finished
a new bow of yew, the best wood.
He had started new arrows, from shoots
of the wayfaring tree. He had almost reached
the pass that herdsmen have used
some five thousand years.

Because he did not survive, he survives.

Note: This poem is based on the 1994 *Man in the Ice* by Dr. Konrad Spindler. Later Italian research with multidimensional X-rays confirmed Spindler's belief that the Iceman died while fleeing human attackers: an arrowhead, shot from behind or below, was found embedded under his left shoulder blade.

## Post-Concussion, Breaking Down

Stone in my hand, small
curved and fossil-broken
river stone, white,
eroded, chill. Outside
the sleeping B & B
I claim you from the cairn
made by our bangled hosts
whose faiths I partway share.
A spider scouts the cairn,
retreats, its cliff-face gone.
A door, far off. Then stillness,
shadow hold us.
                                        Your small weight
comforts me, your smooth
hand-shielded shape. The child's
skull turning in my womb
some thirty years ago,
before she came to light.
The broken mammal skull
I found in the wetland paths
at home, the fur and jaw
dragged farther back. Bright paths,
small seeping tracks. Now I trace
your stone-webbed fossil caves,
where something older lived
and broke away.
                                        Shapes
of lobes, the overhanging
frontal cliffs that kept
Anasazi safe. Eyeholes
carved from waves of stone,
smooth walls built up from small
free-fallen stones. Chill

shadows, where the dancers filled
the kiva's skull, where we
who never knew those prayers
climbed slowly in. The safe
high socket of a world
that fell away.
                    What lives
in your small caves? A fleck
that moves, a thin grey thread
of spider's work. Grey clouds
unravel, shot with light.
A door, slow steps within
the waking B & B.
Eyes closed, I thumb your smooth
bone lobes, your fissured parts.
Small hardness holding up,
small breaking down.
                    Light spurts
through poplar leaves, a first
awakening strobe. A truck,
and soon more sounds, more harmless
lights that jab like lightning
threads across the eyes,
the brain. Enough. I kneel
to set you in your cairn. Stone,
stone, you can keep your wordless
breaking down. I have my own.

# Let Us Now Praise

the one stubbornly
out in the mid-
morning sun, raking his
leaves down the winter-
drained slope of his yard
to the curb, a shining
new walker set at his
right, and a white
metal chair from the kitchen
guarding his left:

and the one glimpsed
from a hallway, or hidden
by curtains, who day after
night after day, still
makes her good hand
catch hold of the gleaming
triangle that hangs
above her barred bed,
who grimacing lifts
a weight so precarious
three shifts of nurses
can't manage it safely.

# Fairland Care: Voices, Doors

*Put the dirt where dirt belongs*
*You sweetie pie you hear my song*
*You didn't see me long and long*
*Go away where you belong!*

An old woman's voice—is she alone?—
coaxes and taunts; her singsong carries
from one of the many open rooms
to the corner of the home's long hall,
where I scan an oil-spill *Geographic*
and watch the door of one shut room.
Behind me, in the blue-green lounge
TV plays on, too loud, the lulling
boombox of the old, who are wheeled
to watch, or drowse, or dream. I wait
in the hall, so Esther won't be lost
when she leaves her sister's private room.

*You've loved each other seventy years,*
I used to say as I held her hand
to guide her past the doors, the aides,
the visitors who look like friends.
Last week our comfort words broke down—
she didn't nod or smile, till I changed
to *all your lives,* then *a real long time.*

One sister's smart, but left the world
for a voice that rules through her alone.
The other's sane, or used to be—
a therapist, in the years before
Alzheimer's moved into her head.
On good days they can patch a visit:
the smart one smiles and shares her food,

the sane one brings the other out
to meet her friends in the corridor.
On better days their visits last
till Esther wants to leave. On worse,
the imperious voice won't let her in—
or calls for Esther, then casts her out.
Worse or better, the present slips,
and Esther can't say where she's been—
just that we need to find Elaine.

In the hall the voice from a farther room
resumes its taunting schoolyard rhymes:

> *Go take the key go lock the door*
> *You take the cake I can't take more*
> *Put the hurt where hurt belongs*
> *Go away where you belong!*

Did I hear *dirt* or *hurt*? The door
I watch stays shut. Disasters, weather,
pleasures blare from the TV.
In the hall, as in a street, the helped
and helpers pass. I find a *Digest*,
thumb its comfort tales of heroes,
risks, and brave enduring love.

## Heron in Shadowed Waters

*for E. Kalmans, 1919-98*

Above the darkened lake, grey sky,
no sun. The darker shapes of cedars
across the silted depths, the duller
shadows of encircling hills.
The heron that you never saw,
grey winter shape.
                                        Your hand in mine,
I helped you cross the narrow stones
to this island overlook, where children
helped us see the swirling, rising carp
that August day. You said this place
was close to home.
                                        Your hands in mine,
you crossed the shifting shallows
of the living room.
                                        Your swollen hand
still warm in mine, those last grey
sunless hours.
                                  Wind lifts and moves
across the darkened waters, a thousand
thousand shapes of light sweep towards us
like a field of glinting grain, a shining
that is here and gone. The heron stirs, and turns
its wind-torn plumage to the wind,
and waits for stillness that will come.

# The Snake Man Explains

the humane way to capture
a resident four-foot
black snake that was recently
climbing the furnace wall
and vanishing over the ceiling
ducts to somewhere unknown:
*It's easy. Just pin it down*
*behind the head with this right-*
*angle molding—I'll leave you*
*this piece—then you grab*
*the tail quick with your free*
*hand, so it can't whip around,*
*don't worry, it can't choke you.*
*Then you get a good*
*grip at the base of its skull*
*with your hand, it's not*
*aggressive, if you get*
*the right place it can't bite.*
*But if it does don't*
*worry, they're not poisonous,*
*it's not like a dog bite, or human,*
*you just wash it out good*
*with soap and warm water. Don't*
*worry if some of its teeth*
*come out in the bite,*
*they're harmless, like fish*
*teeth, they fall right out.*
*Now I'll leave you this blue*
*laundry bag—it's just cloth,*
*so the snake can breathe—*
*you hold the bag open, drop*
*the snake in, tie up the drawstrings*
*and give us a call. Your snake*

*will be fine, it'll just sleep.*
*I'll come back, soon as I can,*
*and take the snake to a woods*
*where we set things free. The snake'll*
*make a new life for itself,*
*don't worry—you'll hear it moving—*
*it's got a nest somewhere*
*in the ceiling or attic—you'll get it.*

# Pathways

## 1

Breath held, I have thanked in my heart the fox
crossing the wetlands, who stopped in his tracks
and gave back my stare, as if he would trust
one smelling of houses but carrying no weapons.
As if, far back, we were something akin.

I have thanked the deer with two fawns, who waited
long moments, flanks quivering, then lowered her head
to browse, letting her newborn come nearer.
And the snapping turtle, heavy with eggs,
who saw me coming into the garden, swivelled
to face my bare shins, then let me retreat.
I watched from a window while she scraped her nests,
two false and one filled, under the chard.

And the small jeweled snake stretched out in the juniper,
who eyed me, deciding, and slowly flowed on.
And the skinny, blue-black wasps in the attic,
drowsily leaving their nest while I waited
to seal off their opening. And so many others—
bees cruising the compost, hawk on the car roof
waiting for prey—I give thanks for their curiosity,
their courage, their wordless patience with us.

## 2

Even the yellow jackets who claimed the boxwood
beside the front steps let us come and go
that summer, let the old cat drowse on his cushion
under their nest. Let me trowel and plant
while they came and went in the dappled light.
Once, when I dropped the toolbox, a few workers
came buzzing, not stinging; they let me sit back,
then mulch the last of our flowering border.

Till the day when the lawn-care mower came roaring
too close to their flyway, spraying green clippings
under their nest. I was off in the wetlands,
avoiding the noise; by the time I came home
the mower was roaring next door. Disgusted,
I reached down to slide the mess of cut grass
off the cat's bed. They had to attack.
It wasn't their fault. No one knew I'd react.

After the shockwaves, the ER, the doctors, I called
the expert, a gentle-voiced guy who grows
organic apples and plums. *Sorry,*
*there's no way to smoke them, no, you can't*
*drive them out with a hose.* I watched from the window
as he sprayed the poison through a twenty-foot tube,
then beat the nest with a rod for stragglers.

### 3

We moved the boxwood, planted things that don't bloom
or hold nests by the entries, soaped the doorframes
where mud daubers had built their grey tubes. Now we check
for new nests by the mailbox, the trash cans, the car.

They still let me watch, with my gloves and sting kit,
as they fly in and out, gold wisps in the sunlight,
small blurs in the shade of the driveway laurels.
It isn't their fault when I phone for their deaths.

This year new wrens feed from our sill
while outsize machines take down the trees
on the edge of the wetlands. Fox, deer,
scalebearers still share their pathways with us—
in need, or ignorance, or something like trust.

## Seeing Is Believing

In the light between shadows,
in the grass between houses and woods,
the orange deer with one good antler,
two points on the left, stands ready to leap,
tense flanks rippling, head lowered,
half-turned to the neighbor's cat who stalks him,
ears flat, spine low in the grass, keeping
one deer leap away. What staring young
animals they are, caught between danger
and play, unsure of their place
on this peaceable slope. Cat sinks down
in the grass, its hunter's tail lashing
and lashing, its haunch weight shifting
as it readies to spring—then settles, chews grass.
Deer waits and waits, looks away at last
to nuzzle the grapevine that smothers
a young cherry beside it. When deer starts chewing
cat moves in a rush like an arrow—deer
leaps backwards and sideways, stops,
sidesteps to circle the cat, still hoping
for a game they can play, still keeping
one deer leap apart. Cat waits, looks elsewhere,
ears up, till some rustling or flutter
pulls it to life—cat races
past deer, disappears in underbrush.
Deer quivers, gives up and grazes.

I still want to believe, like that Quaker painter,
in open green clearings where no one is prey,
where light streams down like palpable grace,
where even the animals—green-eaters, blood-hunters—
lie down believing, lion with lamb.

## Priorities

*She's hung pretty high, your oak. Stay behind me,* says Roy,
*that's eighty feet up where she's caught, in that hickory—see*
*how it's already started to crack? Where's your property line?*
*We'll drop her through here if we can, and spare your azaleas—*
*but a tree like that could split or spin out anytime—*
*I know a guy who's wearing a brace forever.*
*We can't climb her at all, can't rope her worth spit.*
*Tim, the one with the chainsaw, he'll do what he can.*
*Tim called me 4:30 this morning—he's a friend from way back—*
*Did I have work? Do I ever, me and my cousin*
*got trees out our ears with this storm, and Tim's a great climber.*
*We thank you for waiting, but I got priorities—*
*people with trees on their houses and driveways come first.*

It's Tim who walks up to the base of the slanting oak,
beside the ropes that Roy and his cousin have tossed
and fished round the trunk, before they backed off up the hill.
It's Tim, bent over, who cradles the chainsaw, touches down
and pulls back, touch wood and pull back, it looks as easy
as a knife slicing cake, or a surfer shaving a wave—
I can't see the ripple or splint that changes it all—
why he's leaping backwards in air, kicking out
like a Cossack, almost falling downhill, the chainsaw still
whirring
flung off to one side while he leaps, still facing the tree—
and now we can see how it's moving, it's freed, the crashing
thuds down, bounces and thuds, right where Roy said.

*Tim's a real good friend, and as good with the saw as my cousin,*
says Roy as he figures the bill. *But John's my cousin,*
*that's family, you see, and family stays back with the ropes.*

# At the Bronze-Age Citadel

Here where so much has happened
not much will happen again.

We pass unchallenged through the gate of lions,
shaking the dust from our tourist sandals,
presenting our swordless, shieldless sides
to the chambers guarding colossal walls
nine chariots thick, nine chariots high.
Empty these three thousand years.

We circle the stone-ringed burial shaft
where a gold face mask of the beardless king
was found with bits of skin attached—
the king now proved not Agamemnon
but of earlier lineage, long unsung,
whose gleaming mask lives on.

We are led past doorless, roofless shapes
of store room, throne room, altar-scar.
We climb worn steps to the highest place
where kings slept safe, a stair so turned
one warrior could hold off a score.
Stub teeth of stones, still warm.

Outside, beyond the sortie gate,
I take a path that wanders back
to an earlier fort and altar space,
a rise of stones from a time so bleak
that only the ants seek treasure here,
only the dust restores.

Yet someone has scythed these thistles and grains,
laid down the bright sheaves like spears after battle.

Someone has heaped the narrow white shells
of a small land snail, gleaned from the ruins,
as if they were offerings, or a fleet of white hulls
becalmed in a windless gulf.

Sunlight and clouds scour the dark plain.
From the heights the old stories drift down
like gods taking shape in a blind man's song.
I take three shells in my hand, and descend.

# After Long Flight

Who knows where joy first was, or next will be?

After those hours of night becoming grey day,
the long flight home passing over the ever-lit cities,
the last sleeping cliffs like map-shapes fading,
we saw, as we climbed through clouds in aquarial light,
our plane's shadow float like a toy on cloud banks below,
riding the wave-troughs, the fathoms, the risings.

How many time zones, breached in our sleep, go under
before light slants on my face, and yours, and below us
the earth takes shape, white waves on our new-found shore?

Then the tiny old man in a frayed Chinese suit
across from us, alone and bent in his waiting,
quietly raised the white pasteboard box from his lap
to the amber light in the plane's scarred window,

and finches sang out, unseen, and his grey wrinkled face
eased with their song, and we and others
were washed with his joy, though he never looked up from his
    place.

How could we thank him?
                                        He passed through the terminal doors
bearing his treasure before him, rapt as a boy
given charge of a lantern or torch, to show his elders
the path that leads through darkness to a full summer lake.

# November, Ravine Behind Houses

*Owls court in autumn, mate in winter.*

In the slowing year, in the slowly turning night
we wake to stars and the deep blurred calls
of the great horned owl in our neighbor's pines:
unseen, her eight quick pulsing beats
enfold his childless, widowed sleep.

Out back, in the pool of sky where a D-moon rides,
old cuttlebones of cloud dissolve.
We move in shade past hidden lives:
will the owl in her tree-crown depths
accept our slow unknowing steps?

At the world's deep pole, the grounding ice lets go,
the sea floor's unseen depths float free,
the great ice sheet reverts to floe
and flowing seas, the teeming ice-fed life
retreats, pushed back by warmer lives.

Father who mapped the planet's crust and drift,
you have gone back into the earth.
Mother who gathered us when earth's faults slipped,
you have gone back. And yet are here,
in drifts of cloud and flowing earth.

Night pours towards the continent's western rim
as these stars fade. The child we woke
to see the D-moon spell his name
will wake his child where fault lines slip
slowly under younger slopes.

Somewhere beyond our sight the great owl calls,
and her soft membrane resonance
is echoed by a male's quick calls,
five beats across the dark ravine
where builders left a fringe of trees.

# ABOUT THE CAPITAL COLLECTION

The CAPITAL COLLECTION is an imprint by The Word Works that features excellence in poetry from authors in the Greater Washington, DC area. The hallmark of this series is that each book selected is financially supported by advance book sales and community contributions. The author also agrees to work with the press to promote the Capital Collection books, support other activities of The Word Works, and increase public interest in poetry.

The following individuals and organizations have contributed to the Capital Collection to make this book possible:

PATRONS: Daniel M. Benjamin & Mark Braun
Miles David Moore • Hilary Tham

DONORS: Karren Alenier • Mel Belin
Cassandra Benjamin • Martin B. Bernstein
Nadean Bishop & Sheryl Palmer • Lee Blizman
W. Perry Epes • Eli Flam • Virginia Grandison
Paul E. Grayson • Ann B. Knox • Judy Neri
Jeneva Stone • Barbara A. Tenenbaum

FRIENDS: Lorraine Anderson • Barri Armitage
Shuli Barzilai • Christopher Conlon
Gay Hill • Karen Levenback •Paul Napier
John R. Reed • Carol Russel • Carolyn See
Mr. & Mrs. John M. Sheehy • Roseanne Singer
Lee Thompson • Dr. Reginald Wilson
Helen Zucker

We also thank the anonymous contributors who have generously supported this book and the Capital Collection.

## ABOUT THE AUTHOR

Photo by Ernst Benjamin

JUDITH McCOMBS grew up in almost all the continental states, in a geodetic surveyor's family. She has published poetry and short-short fiction in *Calyx, Feminist Studies, Grrrrr: A Collection of Poems about Bears, Kansas Quarterly, Nimrod* (Neruda Award), *Poet Lore, Poetry, Poetry Northwest, Potomac Review* (Poetry Prize), *Prairie Schooner, Prism, River Styx, Sisters of the Earth, Sun Dog,* and elsewhere.

She has held an NEH Fellowship, a Canadian Embassy Senior Fellowship, and a Maryland State Arts Council Award in Poetry; and taught at Wayne State University, as a Creative Writer in the Schools, and at Detroit's Center for Creative Studies College of Art and Design. She is the founding editor of *Moving Out*, which survived for three decades as the nation's second oldest feminist literary magazine. She has published *Critical Essays on Margaret Atwood* and *Margaret Atwood: A Reference Guide* (G. K. Hall). Her creative books are *Sisters and Other Selves* (Glass Bell, MI), 20/20 *Visionary Eclipse & the Whorling Try/ Angles* (Wineberry, DC), *Against Nature: Wilderness Poems* (Dustbooks, CA), and *Territories, Here & Elsewhere* (Mayapple, MI).

She teaches at the Writer's Center in Bethesda, MD, and arranges the Kensington Row Bookshop poetry readings.

## ABOUT THE ARTIST

JOANN CLAYTON TOWNSEND has exhibited internationally in India, Turkey, and through the State Department's *Art in the Embassies*; nationally at the Foundry Gallery, Torpedo Factory, Ratner Museum, and Yellow Barn Gallery. A former Director of the Aeronautics and Space Engineering Board at the National Academy of Sciences, and a Fellow of the American Institute of Aeronautics and Astronautics, she often paints impressions of the cosmos.

See her work at **www.foundrygallery.com**.

# ABOUT THE WORD WORKS

THE WORD WORKS, a nonprofit literary organization, publishes contemporary poetry in collectors' editions. Since 1981, the organization has sponsored the Washington Prize, a $1,500 award to an American poet. Monthly, The Word Works presents free literary programs in the Chevy Chase Café Muse series, and each summer, free poetry programs are held at the historic Joaquin Miller Cabin in Washington, DC's Rock Creek Park. Annually, two high school students debut in the Miller Cabin Series as winners of the Young Poets Competition.

Since 1974, Word Works programs have included: "In the Shadow of the Capitol," a symposium and archival project on the African-American intellectual community in segregated Washington, DC; the Gunston Arts Center Poetry Series (Ai, Carolyn Forché, Stanley Kunitz, and others); the Poet-Editor panel discussions at the Bethesda Writer's Center (John Hollander, Maurice English, Anthony Hecht, Josephine Jacobsen, and others); Poet's Jam, a multi-arts program series featuring poetry in performance; a poetry workshop at the Center for Creative Non-Violence (CCNV) shelter; and the Arts Retreat in Tuscany. Master Class workshops, an ongoing program, have featured Agha Shahid Ali, Thomas Lux, and Marilyn Nelson.

In 2005, Word Works will have published 57 titles, including work from such authors as Deirdra Baldwin, J.H. Beall, Christopher Bursk, John Pauker, Edward Weismiller, and Mac Wellman. Currently, The Word Works publishes books and occasional anthologies under three imprints: the Washington Prize, the Capital Collection, and International Editions.

Past grants have been awarded by the National Endowment for the Arts, National Endowment for the Humanities, DC Commission on the Arts & Humanities, Witter Bynner Foundation, Writer's Center, Bell Atlantic, Batir Foundation, and others, including many generous private patrons.

THE WORD WORKS has established an archive of artistic and administrative materials in the Washington Writing Archive housed in the George Washington University Gelman Library.

Please enclose a self-addressed, stamped envelope with all inquiries.

THE WORD WORKS PO Box 42164 Washington, DC 20015
editor@wordworksdc.com www.wordworksdc.com